Explore

Day and night

by Henry Pluckrose

W
FRANKLIN WATTS
LONDON • SYDNEY

Author's note

This book is one of a series which has been designed to encourage young readers to think about the everyday concepts that form part of their world. The text and photographs complement each other, and both elements combine to provide starting points for discussion. Although each book is complete in itself, each title links closely with others in the set, so presenting an ideal platform for learning.

I have consciously avoided 'writing down' to my readers. Young children like to know the 'real' words for things, and are better able to express themselves when they can use correct terms with confidence.

Young children learn from the experiences they share with adults around them. The child offers his or her ideas which are then developed and extended through the adult. The books in this series are a means for the child and adult to share informal talk, photographs and text, and the ideas which accompany them.

One particular element merits comment. Information books are also reading books. Like a successful story book, an effective information book will be turned to again and again. As children develop, their appreciation of the significance of fact develops too. The young child who asks 'Why do we need clocks?' may subsequently and more provocatively ask, 'Who invented time?' Thoughts take time to generate. Hopefully books like those in this series provide the momentum for this.

Henry Pluckrose

Contents

The sun is a ball
of hot, burning gas.
The sun gives light
and warmth to our earth.

When the sun lights up
the part of the earth
where you are,
it is day-time.

When the sun does not light up
the part of the earth
where you are,
it is night-time.

At night, the moon
reflects light from the sun.
It is like a mirror.

The sun is a giant star.
There are millions of
other stars in the sky, too.
During the day,
the light from the sun
is so bright that we cannot
see these other stars.

In summer, the sun gives us light for longer than in the winter. Midsummer day is the longest day of the year. In some countries it is celebrated with dancing and parties.

In winter, the nights
are longer and darker
than in the summer.
There are lots of
winter celebrations, too.
Can you think of any?

Day-time begins when
the sun rises in the sky.
Sunrise, daybreak and dawn
are all words we use
to describe this.

Most people work
during the day-time.
It is much easier for this farmer
to care for his animals
when it is light.

Day-time ends
when the sun sets and
we can no longer see it.
Nightfall and sunset are words
we use to describe this.

As the day light fades,
electric lights are switched on
to help us see.
At night, lights can make
buildings and statues
look very beautiful.

Some people have to work during the night-time.
What jobs can you think of where people work through the night?

Some animals are nocturnal.
This means that they
stay awake during the night,
and sleep during the day.

Most people rest through
the hours of the night.
They sleep and dream
and wait for a new day to begin.

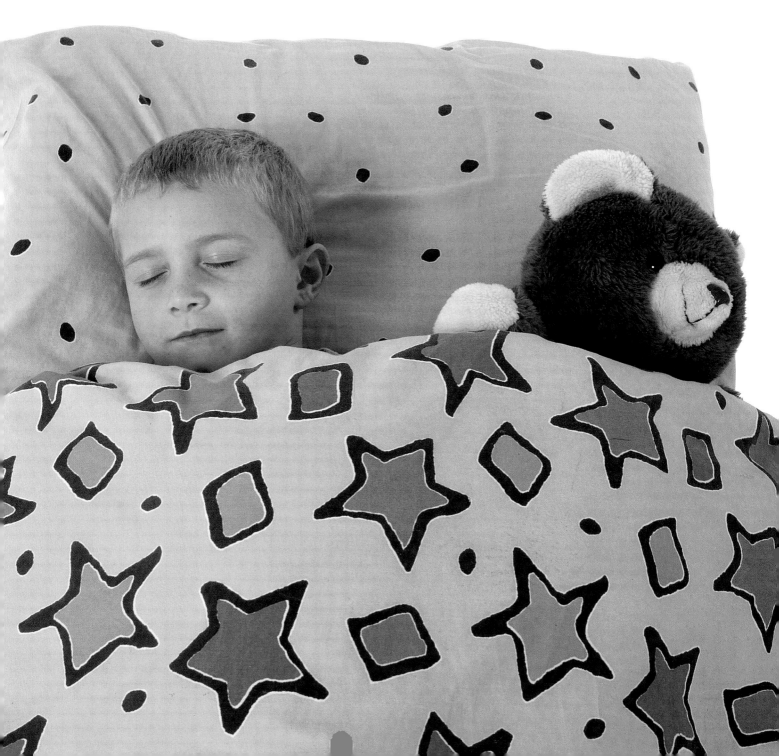

Index

This edition 2004
First published in 2000 by
Franklin Watts
96 Leonard Street
London EC2A 4XD

Franklin Watts Australia
45-51 Huntley Street
Alexandria NSW 2015

Copyright © Franklin Watts 2000

Series editor: Louise John
Series designer: Jason Anscomb

A CIP catalogue record for this book is available from the British Library

Dewey Decimal Classification Number 529

ISBN 0 7496 5644 1

Picture Credits:
Steve Shott Photography, cover page; Ray Moller Photography p. 31; Science Photo Library pp. 4 (Chris Butler), 19 (Geoff Tompkinson); Robert Harding pp. 6 (Roy Rainford), 9 (Nigel Francis), 17 (A. Woolfitt), 25 (Roy Rainford), 27; Bruce Coleman pp. 10 (Kim Taylor), 12 (Astrofoto), 23 (Uwe Walz), 28 (George McCarthy); Eye Ubiquitous p. 15 (James Davis Travel Photography); Oxford Scientific Films p. 20 (Edward Parker).

Printed in China